Original title:
Behind Closed Doors

Editor: Theodor Taimla
Author: Rachelle Randvee
ISBN HARDBACK: 978-9916-763-48-3
ISBN PAPERBACK: 978-9916-763-49-0

Shadows of Silence

Silent whispers in the night,
Echoes caught in moonlight's net.
Dreams that shimmer out of sight,
Secret truths we can't forget.

Softly tread on paths unseen,
Followed by a lone regret.
Memories where we've once been,
In silence, our hopes are met.

A twilight shadow on the wall,
Silent steps in empty halls,
The night is where past dreams fall,
Yet silence sings and heart calls.

Silent voices in the dark,
Carrying stories untold.
Each one leaves a hidden mark,
In the shadows, secrets hold.

Locked Away

In chambers where the echoes sigh,
Dreamscapes of the hidden heart.
Locked away from passersby,
Where the quiet plays its part.

Heavy keys and rusted locks,
Guarding secrets, soft and dear.
Mysteries beneath time's clocks,
Whispered words we hardly hear.

Locked away in deep recess,
Heartfelt whispers come alive.
Each secret in its own dress,
Inside minds where dreams survive.

Beneath the weight of iron doors,
Stories wait so patiently.
Keeping track of silent scores,
In locked rooms of memory.

Private Echoes

Echoes of the mind's own song,
Whispered truth in every note.
Private thoughts where dreams belong,
In the silence, stories float.

In the cavern of the heart,
Secrets form an unseen thread.
Each one crafted, set apart,
In the echoes, softly said.

Private echoes softly trail,
Through the chambers of the mind.
Leaving traces in the veil,
Of the past and time combined.

Yet these whispers hold us near,
Faint and quiet, they remain.
In private echoes, disappear,
Silent truths that softly reign.

In the Quiet Rooms

In the quiet rooms we find,
Refuge from the day's unrest.
Silent moments soothe the mind,
In this calm, we feel most blessed.

Windows open to the sky,
Light pours in with gentle grace.
In these rooms, our spirits fly,
Finding peace in time and space.

Quiet corners, soft and still,
Where the heart lays down its bribes.
Here we drink the quiet's fill,
Surrender to the calm vibes.

In the quiet rooms we dream,
Of tomorrow's gentle flow.
In silence, thoughts start to stream,
Where the seeds of courage grow.

The Private Sphere

Within the walls of silent rooms,
From weary day to twilight's bloom,
Thoughts unspoken, whispers glide,
In shadows where our secrets hide.

Curtains drawn, the night's descent,
Softly cloaks each sentiment,
In quietude, we find a space,
Where dreams and fears in tandem chase.

Books unopened, letters sealed,
A world within, thoughts unreeled,
Memories woven, moments near,
Are cradled in the private sphere.

Heartbeats echo in the still,
Time suspended by sheer will,
In solitude, our souls appear,
Unmasked within the private sphere.

Through unseen threads, emotions weave,
A tapestry of night's reprieve,
In silence, voices hold sincere,
The echoes of the private sphere.

Hidden Facades

Beneath the masks that smile and bow,
Lies truth unseen by eye or vow,
A play of shadows, light conceals,
The hidden facades no glance reveals.

Mirror's gaze but scratches thin,
The surface where deceptions spin,
With guards erect on heart’s high walls,
Disguising pain when silence calls.

Words articulate a crafted tale,
Yet behind the visage, secrets pale,
In passageways of guarded minds,
The true self waits as reason binds.

Voices low in quiet refrain,
Discourses wrap around the pain,
Beneath the laugh and courteous nod,
Lie hidden facades that thoughts applaud.

In labyrinths of social grace,
Are fragments of the inner space,
Each fragmented, poorly shod,
The hidden facades of self’s applaud.

Hidden Whispers

Amid the autumn's gentle breeze,
A susurrus of leaves and trees,
Lies whispers hid from prying ears,
Enfolded soft, dispelling fears.

In twilight's hush, they intertwine,
With secrets shared, and dreams benign,
A language written in the air,
That lingers sweetly, unaware.

The nightingale's soft melody,
Is but a whisper birthed by sea,
Of endless tales and silent pleas,
That flit upon the evening's ease.

In cracks of silence, murmurs dwell,
Invisible yet cast their spell,
For those who listen with their hearts,
Unlock the whispers' fragile parts.

Through shadows cast on moonlit land,
They glide so light, a ghostly hand,
Unseen, unheard by heedless minds,
Yet whisper truths that time refines.

Veiled Murmurs

In twilight's arms, the murmurs soft,
Veiled beneath the stars aloft,
A chorus faint that whispers low,
In shadows where the secrets grow.

Ephemeral as morning mist,
They touch the soul with gentle twist,
Invisible to waking minds,
Yet palpable in silent kinds.

Beneath the moon's watchful eye,
Veiled murmurs drift and multiply,
Each one a note in night's refrain,
A haunting, melancholic strain.

In dreams they dance with silent grace,
Across the fields of night's embrace,
Unfurling tales with every breeze,
Of ancient loves and memories.

And as the dawn begins to rise,
They fade into the brightening skies,
Veiled murmurs, whispering once more,
Return to night, where shadows soar.

Secrets of the Night

Under the moon's soft, silvery gaze,
Whispers dance in shadowy haze.
Stars play hide and seek with dreams,
Night uncovers what daylight screens.

Beneath the veil of twilight's breath,
Mysteries breathe, defying death.
Owls sing songs of ancient lore,
Silent secrets forevermore.

The forest sighs, a gentle hymn,
Leaves in dark, a phantom limb.
Crickets chirp their midnight tale,
Winds of wonder softly wail.

In the hush, where shadows blend,
Unknown truths begin to mend.
Midnight cloaks the whispered fright,
Revealing secrets of the night.

Hidden Agendas

Behind a smile, a hidden plan,
Crafted by a clever hand.
Words that in the daylight gleam,
Hide the shadows unseen scheme.

In the corridors of power,
Pawns are played hour by hour.
Trust is but a fleeting guest,
In the hearts, where secrets rest.

Promises are woven tight,
Underneath the guise of right.
Watch the players in their stance,
Moving pieces in the dance.

Eyes that glitter in the dusk,
Masking motives, shrouded, husk.
In the silence, plots unfurl,
Hidden agendas shape the world.

Caged Dreams

In a cage of iron bars,
Dreams imprisoned, bleak and charred.
Wings of hope they try to raise,
Trapped within the shadowed maze.

Eyes that long for skies of blue,
Hungering for vistas new.
Hands that reach from out the night,
Grasping for the morning light.

Yet within the heart's deep core,
Flickers dreams of something more.
Even in the darkened frame,
Whispers call the dreamer’s name.

Time and tide might wear them thin,
But caged dreams dwell deep within.
Hope rekindles soft and small,
Until the bars begin to fall.

Silent Screams

In the quiet of the night’s embrace,
Silent screams find their place.
Voices hushed, unheard by day,
Echo in the dark’s array.

Pain concealed behind a mask,
Questions that no one dares to ask.
Whispers linger in the air,
Silent screams of deep despair.

Through the stillness, shadows creep,
Secrets that the heart will keep.
Eyes reflecting untold pain,
Voiceless cries, a hidden chain.

In the somber, starlit dreams,
Lies the truth of silent screams.
One more hope, a breath away,
Holds the dawn of a new day.

Whispered Worlds

In twilight's calm, the whispers start,
A secret breath, a hidden art.
They twine through air and touch the heart,
In murmurs soft, they take their part.

Through shadowed glens, they gently sweep,
A song of dreams within our sleep.
In whispered worlds where secrets keep,
The silent vows we dare to reap.

The moonlight casts its silver thread,
On whispered paths where footsteps tread.
In realms of quiet, softly spread,
Where thoughts like whispers are gently fed.

The stars above, in chorus sing,
A harmony on cosmic wing.
In whispered worlds where hopes do cling,
The voiceless truths are echoing.

Curtained Realities

Behind the veil, a realm unseen,
In curtained folds, where shadows glean.
A dance of dreams in silver sheen,
Where hidden truths await between.

The whispers of a nameless song,
In curtained worlds where we belong.
An echoing of time so long,
In silent echoes, clear and strong.

Soft gestures in the twilight fade,
In curtained realms where thoughts invade.
A whispered spell that dreams have made,
In silent nights, beneath the shade.

The mind and heart in secret play,
In curtained worlds where shadows sway.
The hidden paths where thoughts do lay,
In silent depths, a muffled day.

Veil of Silence

Beneath the still, a silence grows,
In veils that shift where silence flows.
The quiet shade, a calm repose,
In whispering winds, a secret knows.

A veil of silence softly falls,
In hidden halls where quiet calls.
The muted echoes of these walls,
In silent breath, the stillness stalls.

In silent nights, the stars confide,
Through veils of silence, shadows glide.
In whispered dreams where hopes reside,
A silent journey, side by side.

The veil of silence softly sways,
In tranquil mists where silence lays.
With whispered light of ending days,
In silent whispers, the heart obeys.

Solitary Reveries

In solitude, the dreams unfold,
A reverie where thoughts are gold.
In quiet moments, secrets told,
In whispers soft and hearts so bold.

A solitary path, alone,
With shadows cast on dreams unknown.
The quiet steps where thoughts have flown,
In reveries where seeds are sown.

In twilight's calm, the mind retreats,
To solitary, silent beats.
A world within where heart completes,
In reveries, the soul repeats.

The quietude of night surrounds,
In solitary, dreamlike grounds.
With whispered hopes that know no bounds,
In reveries where peace is found.

Silent Hallways

In the stillness of the night,
Silent hallways breathe in peace.
Shadows dance with muted light,
In this hush, all echoes cease.

Footsteps fade like drifting snow,
Ghostly whispers softly sing.
Memories in soft winds blow,
Silent secrets they will bring.

Moonlight spills through window's grace,
Silhouettes of thoughts unknown.
In this tranquil, sacred space,
Silent hallways stand alone.

Every creak and wooden moan,
Tell a tale from ages gone.
In this realm, we're not alone,
Silent shadows linger on.

Clandestine Paths

Through the woods where secrets dwell,
Clandestine paths meander slow.
Mysteries they weave and tell,
Of forgotten tales they know.

Mossy stones and ancient trees,
Guard the whispers of the past.
Here, the spirits find their ease,
Where the shaded trails are cast.

Footprints lost in verdant sea,
Echoes from another time.
In the hush of secrecy,
Silent stories subtly chime.

Tread with caution, tread with care,
On these paths by moonlight's bath.
For the magic lingers there,
On clandestine, hidden paths.

Shaded Realities

Behind the veil of day's bright gleam,
Shaded realities arise.
Blending truth with whispered dream,
In the dark where silence lies.

Mirrors show a fractured face,
Reflections not of what we see.
In the shadows, time and space,
Warp their way through mystery.

Silent corners hide the hues,
Of a world not often known.
Underneath the sky’s dark blues,
Shaded truths have softly grown.

In the twilight's tender grasp,
Hold to what you think is real.
Shaded realms can often clasp,
All that's hidden, all you feel.

Veiled Dreams

In the quiet of the night,
Veiled dreams like whispers come.
Misted visions taking flight,
In this world where stars are numb.

Secrets held beneath closed eyes,
Wander through the mind's soft maze.
In the land where silence flies,
Dreams are clothed in moonlit haze.

Thoughts adrift in silent seas,
Float on tides of what might be.
In the mirror of the breeze,
Veiled dreams unveil silently.

Each heart holds a hidden truth,
Buried deep within its gleam.
In the mysteries of youth,
Lie the whispers of each dream.

Veiled Realities

In shadows where the whispers lie,
A world unseen begins to sigh
Behind the veil of what we see,
Exists a realm of mystery.

A fleeting glance, a hidden clue,
Uncovers secrets old and new,
We walk through veiled realities,
Entwined in life's complexities.

The night unveils its sacred dance,
A silent, spectral, dark romance,
Yet in the murmur of the breeze,
Lie truths disguised in harmonies.

The morning light, a fragile hope,
Empowers minds to truly cope,
With veiled realities around,
In every sigh, a deeper sound.

Beyond what eyes could ever tell,
In hidden realms we often dwell,
Our dreams reveal reality,
In whispers of eternity.

The Locked Room

A room enshrouded, locked away,
Within its walls, mere shadows play,
Lost secrets echo, soft and clear,
In silence, whispers we can hear.

The key to worlds we cannot see,
Lies deep in hidden memory,
In this enclosure, time stands still,
A space where dreams and fears fulfill.

Each crack and crevice tells a tale,
Of moments lost and lives so frail,
Yet in this room, we find a spark,
Of timeless light within the dark.

A mystery behind the door,
Awaiting those who seek for more,
For in the quiet, hearts may race,
To find what lies in secret place.

The locked room holds a cryptic code,
A path where only few have strode,
Within its still and whispered gloom,
We find the truth within the room.

Silent Echoes

In the stillness of the night,
Silent echoes take their flight,
Whispers hidden, lost in time,
Resonating through the chime.

Voices linger in the air,
With stories old they softly share,
Unheard murmurs fill the space,
With memories we can't erase.

In the hush of nature's call,
Silent echoes tell it all,
Every leaf and breath of wind,
Speaks of places hearts have been.

In the silence, hear the past,
Echoes of a love that lasts,
Timeless whispers, soft, refined,
In our hearts forever bind.

Listen close and hear the sound,
Of silent echoes all around,
They weave a tale both strange and true,
Of endless dreams and skies so blue.

Clandestine Murmurs

In secret meetings of the mind,
Clandestine murmurs we may find,
Words unspoken, thoughts profound,
In shadows' whispers, truth is found.

Behind the veil of every day,
Lie murmurs hidden, tucked away,
Silent voices, words so clear,
In the quiet, we can hear.

Lives entwined in secret streams,
Clandestine murmurs speak in dreams,
A tapestry of unseen threads,
Connecting hearts and quiet dreads.

In twilight's hush, where worlds collide,
These murmurs whisper, truth and pride,
In secrets shared and confidences,
Lies the strength of pure alliances.

The night reveals a sacred trust,
In murmurs soft, without a fuss,
Clandestine secrets we discern,
In whispers, silent truths we learn.

Occulted Truths

In shadows deep where secrets lie,
The hidden truths, they pass us by.
With whispered winds and moonlit beams,
The night unfolds its shadowed dreams.

Mysteries draped in darkened veils,
Stories told in hushed exhales.
A dance of silence, cryptic cues,
Unlocking these occulted truths.

Echoes of ages, ancient lore,
Guardians of the secrets' core.
Riddles wrapped in twilight’s hue,
Yet we seek what’s always true.

Secret Corners

In corners dark, where shadows meld,
Untold stories softly held.
A quiet place where whispers stay,
In secret corners tucked away.

Hidden realms and subtle lights,
Guarded well from prying sights.
The silence speaks in softest tones,
A world where mystery roams.

Time stands still and moments linger,
Secrets held by unseen fingers.
Embrace the quiet, hold it near,
In these corners, nothing's clear.

Shrouded Mysterious

In the mist of dawn's first breath,
The shrouded path leads to unknown.
A world where mystery dances free,
And truth is rarely ever shown.

Veils of shadows, cloaks of night,
Guarded secrets, out of sight.
A labyrinth of doubt and awe,
The shrouded mystery's silent law.

Glimpses of the hidden past,
Moments that we hold steadfast.
We walk the line 'tween known and veiled,
In search of truths eternally hailed.

Under Lock and Key

Behind the door, beneath the seal,
Lies a secret none reveal.
Guarded closely, watched with care,
Safe from those who’d badly fare.

Key in hand with purpose clear,
Mysteries held so dear.
Questions whisper, answers tease,
Locked away with subtle ease.

Seekers ponder, search and pry,
Still, the secrets slyly lie.
Under lock and key they rest,
In the hearts where truth is blessed.

The Quiet Room

In the quiet room of thought, we find,
A place where echoes whisper, minds.
Silent tales of dreams untold,
In shadows, mysteries unfold.

The window frames the morning light,
Softly breaks the still of night.
Each beam a letter, each ray a word,
In the quiet room, no sound's disturbed.

Shelves bear witness, oaths of books,
Words in slumber, thoughtful looks.
History rests 'neath covered shade,
In the quiet room, stories laid.

A candle flickers, dances slow,
Warmth emerges, gentle glow.
Unspoken secrets find their tomb,
In the soft embrace, the quiet room.

There in the hush, our hearts align,
Silence speaks in lines divine.
Moments frozen, time resumes,
In the gentle calm, the quiet room.

Hearts Concealed

Beneath the veils of silent night,
Hearts concealed from common sight.
Whispers kept in shadows hide,
Emotions deep, though none confide.

Masked by smiles, concealed deftly,
Feelings twine so intricately.
Tender echoes faintly feel,
In the stillness, hearts conceal.

Eyes may wander, lips may part,
Yet hidden stays the deepest heart.
Veins of love through whispers steal,
In the quiet, hearts conceal.

Behind the laughter, under breath,
Love persists, defying death.
Unrevealed, in dreams they heal,
Wrapped in night, hearts conceal.

Invisible threads bind the soul,
In the silence, hearts console.
Unseen currents strong and real,
In the darkened veil, hearts conceal.

Invisible Battles

In the silence, wars are waged,
Invisible battles fiercely staged.
Unseen scars that lie within,
In hearts, the storms and tempest spin.

Eyes reflect a calm refrain,
Yet beneath, there lurks the pain.
Silent struggles, minds assail,
Invisible battles, tales unveil.

No warrior's cry, no trumpet's call,
Just whispers echo, rise and fall.
In the depths, where shadows wrest,
Invisible battles find no rest.

The soul endures, in quiet night,
Fights the dark to seek the light.
No shields, no swords, no armored chain,
Invisible battles, silent reign.

With every dawn, a new repair,
Hearts renew in morning's air.
In the quiet still, they strive,
Invisible battles, strength revive.

Encased Emotions

Beneath the surface, hearts entwine,
Encased emotions, traces fine.
Locked within a tender grip,
Silent feelings gently slip.

Echoes of the unsaid word,
Flutter like a caged bird.
In the depths where secrets roam,
Encased emotions find their home.

Eyes convey what lips conceal,
Unspoken truths that lovers feel.
A touch, a glance, a fleeting smile,
Encased emotions reconcile.

Through the barriers, strong and clear,
Every heartbeat draws them near.
Veiled thoughts in love's embrace,
Encased emotions, time's embrace.

Silent rivers, deep and wide,
Emotions ebb with every tide.
Hidden worlds, yet intertwined,
Encased emotions, hearts aligned.

Latent Sorrows

In the shadows of twilight's reign,
Silent whispers hold their pain.
Stars look down with distant eyes,
On sorrows hidden in the skies.

A heart beat lost in time's embrace,
Tears unseen leave no trace.
Caught between dusk and dawn,
Mourning whispers softly drawn.

Echoes of a past unspoken,
Fragments of dreams left broken.
In the night where shadows weave,
Latent sorrows take their leave.

Beneath the moon's somber glow,
Memories like rivers flow.
Silent songs of yesteryears,
Tales of sorrows, muted fears.

The quiet night holds its breath,
Listening to tales of death.
Latent sorrows softly sway,
In the heart where shadows play.

Confidential Echoes

In the vaults of whispered minds,
Secrets hidden, truths confined.
Echoes of what once was said,
Dance in silence, filled with dread.

Locked away in chambers deep,
Promises we swore to keep.
Words unsaid, yet clearly known,
In our hearts, they've brightly grown.

Through the corridors they fly,
Confidential, yet they'll pry.
Seeking ears to softly lean,
On the borders of unseen.

In the night where silence speaks,
Confidential echoes peek.
Telling tales of love and woe,
Seeking solace, seeking glow.

Within shadows, secrets blend,
On whispers, they will depend.
Confidential echoes stay,
Haunting hearts by night and day.

Masked Realities

Beneath the facade, truth lies bare,
Masked realities, everywhere.
Glances hide what words imply,
Behind the eyes, the realness shy.

Wearing masks made of clay,
We dance through life, day by day.
Hiding from the world's harsh gaze,
In our masquerade-like haze.

Behind the laughter, silent screams,
In daylight's truth, hidden dreams.
Chasing shadows, chasing light,
Masked realities take flight.

In the mirror, reflections stray,
Truth and illusion often play.
Lies we tell to hide our fears,
Masked realities through the years.

Peel away the layers deep,
Sins and secrets buried heap.
Masked realities unfold,
Stories left untold, retold.

Silent Corners

In the corners where silence stays,
Softly hum the quiet days.
Whispers speak to those who hear,
In the calm, they draw near.

Shadows dance in shaded nooks,
Telling tales in wordless books.
Silent corners hide their lore,
Echoes of what's gone before.

In the stillness, mountains sigh,
Silent corners never die.
Holding breath in time's embrace,
Every secret finds its place.

Where the light and dark entwine,
Silent corners hold the line.
Between the stars and deep abyss,
In their quiet, lies true bliss.

Wander there, in search of peace,
Silent corners never cease.
With their whispers, soft and mild,
Lost realities reconciled.

Private Storms

In quiet nights, the tempest roars,
Within the soul, a war unveils,
No outward sign, no cries or calls,
Yet deep within, the thunder wails.

Silent skies, a placid ruse,
The heart contends with unseen tides,
Beneath the calm, a fierce abuse,
In shadows, inner truth resides.

Through whispered winds, the battles wage,
Invisible, the sleepless fight,
A private storm on hidden stage,
Confined within, beyond the sight.

Unseen Struggles

Beneath the smile, a tale untold,
A weight unseen, a silent plea,
In every heart, a burden bold,
Unseen struggles, wild and free.

In daylight's grace, they mask the pain,
With laughter's veil, they hide the tears,
Yet in their eyes, you see the strain,
The echoes of unspoken fears.

Courage thrives in quiet forms,
Enduring trials, unseen by light,
Their whispered cries, in silent norms,
Are battles fought, beyond our sight.

Hidden Truths

In shadows cast by light's embrace,
Lie truths obscured, in darkness shrouded,
A perfect mask, a flawless face,
Behind the veil, the heart is crowded.

With gentle words, a world conceals,
The hidden truths, within the mind,
In quiet thoughts, the soul reveals,
What spoken words could never find.

In every glance, a secret lies,
In every smile, a story weaves,
Through time's unending enterprise,
The heart's true lore, the mind perceives.

Subtle Deceptions

In whispered tones, the lies are spun,
With gentle touch, deceit begins,
A labyrinth, with threads undone,
Where shadows dance, and light rescinds.

The smile that hides a thousand woes,
The eyes that sparkle, yet deceive,
In subtle ways, the falsehood grows,
A play of trust, we often weave.

Behind the charm, a cunning guise,
The truth is twisted, yet unseen,
In subtle deceptions, perfect lies,
We dwell in webs, through fate's routine.

Whispered Secrets

In twilight's gentle, amber hue,
The whispers of the night ensue,
Soft secrets carried on the breeze,
Rustling through the ancient trees.

Beneath the moon's soft silver glow,
The mysteries of time unfold,
Silent echoes of the past,
Through time's windows, shadows cast.

In each hushed breath the secrets lie,
Of dreams that soar beyond the sky,
Fantastical, enchanting tales,
That ride upon the starlit sails.

Wherever whispers gently sweep,
The heart's profoundest corners keep,
Unspoken, veiled in midnight's kiss,
A waltz of shadows, whispered bliss.

Listen close with keen intent,
To twilight's mystic, soft lament,
For in those whispers, truths we find,
The sealed confessions of the mind.

Enclosed Emotions

In chambers of the heart confined,
Where love and sorrow intertwine,
Silent tears and muted cries,
In hidden corners, feeling lies.

Veins of passion, veins of fear,
Interwoven memories sear,
A tapestry of joy and pain,
In every thread, a new refrain.

Beneath the calmly placid face,
A storm of sentiments embrace,
The tumult of a thousand dreams,
Locked in the heart's secretive schemes.

Feelings sheltered, neatly stored,
Behind the mind's defensive door,
A sanctuary of the soul,
A hidden world, a private whole.

Enclosed emotions softly burn,
In shadows, waiting for their turn,
To break the chains that softly hold,
And let their vibrant stories unfold.

Secluded Worlds

In hidden nooks, the worlds reside,
Unseen beneath the conscious tide,
Where fantasies and dreams entwine,
Beyond the realms of space and time.

Each secluded corner gleams,
With whispered thoughts and silent dreams,
A universe in every mind,
Where endless realms are undefined.

Through the veils of solitude,
Mystic lands in quietude,
Secret paths that lead away,
To realms where fantasies hold sway.

In these worlds the soul is free,
To dance with stars, to kiss the sea,
A land where limits fade and blur,
Reality begins to stir.

Secluded worlds apart from eyes,
Where endless magic softly lies,
Explore the depths within your heart,
And let these worlds of wonder start.

Tales Untold

Among the leaves with stories veined,
Lie tales untold, in silence chained,
Each wrinkle in the tree's old bark,
Holds echoes of a hidden spark.

In shadows cast by rocks and rills,
In whispers of the gentle hills,
Unwritten lines in nature's prose,
Await the pen that never shows.

The ancient winds through valleys weave,
Soft tales that time dares not retrieve,
In every gust, a story's breath,
That fades into the past's deep depths.

Forgotten lore in caverns dark,
And songs that night skies dare not hark,
Lie dormant, waiting to be freed,
By hearts that listen, hearts that heed.

May someday they be softly told,
These whispered dreams and tales of old,
Unlocked from time's relentless hold,
And into eager hearts enfold.

Untold Stories

In whispers of the midnight air,
Tales unfold with silent care,
Unseen by eyes, unheard by ears,
They float like phantoms through the years.

In shadows cast by candlelight,
Words unsaid yet burning bright,
Their echoes haunt the space between,
The spoken and the once unseen.

A tapestry of hidden dreams,
Woven into silent seams,
Narratives of heart and flight,
Ghostly in the darkest night.

Long forgotten, still they roam,
In minds where they have found a home,
Eternal in their quiet grace,
The untold stories find their place.

In every soul, a story's thread,
Seeks a voice and seeks a bed,
To rest within, to be unfurled,
Untold stories of the world.

Under the Surface

Beneath the calm, a tempest brews,
In silence lies the deepest truths,
What's seen above, but masks the waves,
Of hidden depths in secret caves.

Beneath the surface of a smile,
Sorrows sleep and dreams beguile,
A masquerade of daily life,
Conceals the undercurrents' strife.

In tranquil lakes, in calmest seas,
There lies the story no one sees,
Of battles fought and tears unseen,
Below the tranquil, serene sheen.

Unseen by those who skim the frame,
Emotions churn with timeless flame,
Within the depths where few can reach,
Lie truths that few would dare to breach.

So look beyond the surface glaze,
Through silent depths and hidden haze,
For underneath the calm facade,
Are truths that nudge, disrupt, and prod.

Guarded Truths

In silence kept with guarded hearts,
Where shadows fall and light departs,
There lies the truth that none can see,
Locked within a mystery.

With heavy chains and secret keys,
Truths are kept from those who seize,
In fortresses behind the eyes,
Where hidden, deep, the secret lies.

A world within, untouched by light,
Protects the truth with silent might,
Guarded by a whispered vow,
Unseen by all who question how.

And there within the quiet reign,
Guarded truths become the chain,
That bind the soul with unseen force,
And steer the heart upon its course.

Oh, guarded truths with secret might,
Keep within the darkest night,
For only those with keys well-earned,
Will find the truths for which they yearned.

Muffled Cries

In the quiet of the night,
Whispers wrap around the light,
Muffled cries and silenced pleas,
Echo through the unseen seas.

In rooms where no one hears the call,
Silent tears begin to fall,
Shadows dance and shadows play,
As voices fade and drift away.

Within the heart, a muffled beat,
A cadence lost to light and heat,
Cries for help that find no ear,
In the quiet, disappear.

Behind the smile, behind the gaze,
A silent storm begins to blaze,
Unspoken words and hidden sighs,
Reside within the muffled cries.

For every voice that no one hears,
For every cry and silent tears,
There lies a story left untold,
And dreams that falter, lose their hold.

Silent Passages

Whispers trace the bricks of night,
Guided by the soft moon's light.
Footsteps echo, soft and slow,
Through the paths where shadows grow.

Curtains drawn, windows tight,
Guarding secrets, out of sight.
Echoes low, they rise and fade,
In the silent promenade.

Leaves rustle in a sacred dance,
Underneath the stars' cold glance.
Silent whispers float and sweep,
Bearing dreams that shadows keep.

Hushed the voices, faint and near,
In this passage, none shall hear.
Through these corridors we glide,
Where the quiet memories reside.

Silent paths, unseen, unknown,
In the dark, we're not alone.
Here the quiet marks its claim,
On these ways that have no name.

The Hidden Chamber

Deep within the heart of stone,
Lies a secret, sealed, alone.
Walls that whisper tales of old,
Guarding treasures yet untold.

Ancient keys of iron wrought,
Hold the mysteries once sought.
Candles flicker, shadows play,
In this chamber's hidden sway.

Veils of dust on treasures cast,
Echoes from the distant past.
Silent guardians still stand,
In this carved, forgotten land.

Scrolls of wisdom, bound in lore,
Rest unbroken, near the door.
Mysteries in silence lay,
In the dark where memories stay.

Vault of secrets, safely kept,
In this chamber, ages slept.
Hidden truths and silent screams,
Guarded here, within our dreams.

Enclosed Shadows

Darkened corners hide their face,
In the night, they find their place.
Figures moving, silent, still,
In the shadow, breathes the chill.

Wandering in a moonlit maze,
Through the dusk, the shadows glaze.
Silent steps on paths unknown,
In this world, we walk alone.

Hidden whispers in the night,
Shadows dance in pale moonlight.
Cloaked in mist, the fear remains,
In the dark, the silence reigns.

Hollow voices, distant calls,
Echoes in the ancient halls.
Shadows linger, never fade,
In the dark, their forms are made.

Veiled in silence, shadows keep,
In their folds, the secrets sleep.
Watching, waiting, in the gloom,
In the shadows, none presume.

Within the Silence

In the quiet, whispers blend,
Silent messages they send.
Every echo, every sigh,
Tells a tale as moments fly.

Muted wind and stillness merge,
In the silence, feelings surge.
Hidden thoughts begin to speak,
In the hush, minds seek and seek.

Silent stars in navy skies,
Hold the answers, unveil lies.
Within the silence, world's aglow,
Secrets only night can know.

Harmonies of voiceless song,
In the silence, they belong.
Movements trace invisible lines,
In the quiet, truth aligns.

Still moments, softly spun,
Within silence, all is one.
Echoes fade, yet stories rise,
In the quiet, silence lies.

Behind the Latch

A whisper breaks the silent night,
Where mysteries and shadows meet,
A flicker in the dimming light,
Secrets hidden, silence sweet.

The latch clicks tight, a keeper's vow,
Guarding whispers in the dark,
A testament of then and now,
An unseen witness, silent mark.

Echoes dance upon the wall,
Stories trapped within the wood,
Every creek and whispered call,
Tales unknown, misunderstood.

In the stillness, dreams take flight,
Behind the latch, the past lies still,
Whispers held through endless night,
A realm unseen, but never nil.

Locked away from prying sight,
The heart of shadows makes its stand,
Behind the latch, in soft moonlight,
Truth awaits beneath the hand.

Under Lock and Key

Hidden truths in secret places,
Guarded by the sternest locks,
Mysteries upon their faces,
Striking as the midnight clocks.

In the deep and silent corners,
Time stands still, yet seconds flee,
Under watchful eyes of mourners,
Keeping all beneath the key.

Echoes of forgotten stories,
Drift through walls with fervent plea,
Glimpses of the past in glories,
Under lock and unseen key.

Secrets held in rooms of velvet,
Whispered across cold, empty halls,
History's breath felt and smelt,
Behind the iron and thickened walls.

Within silence, shadows linger,
Guardians of what used to be,
Locked away by hidden fingers,
Bound forever, under key.

Inner Sanctum

Deep within the soul's pure core,
Where heartbeats sync and secrets lay,
A world awaits behind the door,
A haven hidden, kept at bay.

Thoughts and dreams both soft and fierce,
Dwell within this sacred ground,
An inner sanctum, none to pierce,
Where truth and solace both are found.

Silent whispers of the mind,
Echo softly 'neath the skin,
Hopes and fears all intertwined,
In the space where thoughts begin.

Sacred moments held so dear,
In the quiet spaces known,
Within where nothing's ever clear,
Yet clarity is softly shown.

The heart's own fortress strong and true,
Holds the essence carefully,
In the inner sanctum's view,
Peace resides eternally.

Shielded Thoughts

Thoughts behind a tempered shield,
Guarded by a watchful eye,
In the space where truths are wield,
Dreams and echoes silent lie.

Steel and stone, a fortress strong,
Hides the whispers, thoughts concealed,
Memories both right and wrong,
In the sanctum unrevealed.

Silent sentinels stand guard,
Over moments held in mind,
Every memory battle-scarred,
Past and present intertwined.

In the depths where shadows play,
Thoughts emerge then slip away,
In the heart where secrets stay,
Safe behind their own array.

Shielded thoughts in quiet keep,
Guard the soul's most fervent dreams,
In the silence, shadows deep,
Silent whispers, hidden themes.

Locked Hearts

Within the chambers, secrets keep,
Whispered words in silence sleep,
Love's embrace and pain's retreat,
Hearts entwined in bonds so deep.

Chains invisible, holding tight,
Dreams concealed in endless night,
Whispers echo, softly glide,
In the shadows, truth resides.

Keys forgotten, rust away,
Locked hearts yearn for light of day,
Glances stolen, moments missed,
Silent tears in moonlight kissed.

In the dark, love finds a way,
Through the night, it seeks the day,
Hope endures, despite the chains,
Locked hearts beating through the pains.

Time may heal, the future bright,
Revealed by morning's gentle light,
Cages open, hearts set free,
Love's pure essence, eternally.

Mysteries Unveiled

In shadows cast by fleeting light,
Secrets hide from piercing sight,
Veils of night, obscured lines,
Mysteries shrouded in the pines.

Ancient echoes whisper near,
Tales of wonder fill the ear,
Truths unspoken, softly hum,
Mysteries unveiled, come undone.

Every fold and every crease,
Holds a fragment of the peace,
Puzzle pieces, twilight gleams,
Mysteries revealed in dreams.

Paths we walk, footsteps trace,
In the labyrinth's embrace,
Unveil the hidden, find the true,
Mysteries unwrapped, born anew.

Stars above, cryptic dance,
Serenading night's romance,
Truth and fiction, hence conjoined,
Mysteries unveiled, souls anoint.

Enclosed Sorrows

Beneath the veil of silent cries,
Sorrows lurk in soft disguise,
Tears like rivers, secrets flow,
In the heart's concealed shadow.

Wounds untended, scars still raw,
Pain unspoken, sorrow's law,
Eyes reflecting, hidden pain,
Enclosed sorrows, endless rain.

Dreams of yesterday now grey,
Withered hopes in night decay,
Silent whispers, empty hands,
Enclosed sorrows, shifting sands.

Walls surround, the heart confined,
Lost in echoes, trapped in time,
Faintest glimmers, softly speak,
Enclosed sorrows, heartstrings weak.

Yet dawn may come with healing light,
Breaking through the endless night,
Hope's embrace to gently mend,
Enclosed sorrows find an end.

Concealed Melancholy

In the quiet of the dawn,
Where whispers of the night are gone,
Melancholy finds its place,
In shadows cast upon the face.

Silent tears that fall unseen,
Hearts that crack in the between,
Smiles that hide the deepest ache,
Concealed melancholy, hearts that break.

Through the laughter, joy appears,
Masking all the hidden fears,
Loneliness within the crowd,
Concealed melancholy, softly vowed.

Eyes that gleam with secret pain,
Memories like the falling rain,
Songs that echo silent cries,
Concealed melancholy, in disguise.

Yet in the core of silent night,
A flicker grows, a spark of light,
Hope that walks the shadowed way,
Concealed melancholy, seeks the day.

Unvoiced Whispers

Through twilight's veil, the shadows creep,
Where secrets form and silence keep.
Unheard, the whispers spread and swell,
In realms where quiet thoughts dwell.

The night enfolds the hidden fears,
In darkness, sorrow sheds its tears.
Unseen by all, the murmurs fade,
Within the hush, the echoes wade.

At dawn, the whispers softly blend,
With morning's light, they find an end.
Yet in the heart, a trace remains,
Of silent whispers' gentle chains.

Among the stars, the dreams descend,
No sound disrupts, no tongues offend.
In cosmic stillness, truths abide,
In unvoiced whispers, depths reside.

So listen close, with inner ear,
For whispers faint that draw you near.
In silence, wisdom softly stirs,
And secrets speak through whispers' purrs.

Covered Secrets

Beneath the earth, in shadows lain,
The secrets hide from light's domain.
Enshrouded deep, away from sight,
They whisper tales of endless night.

In darkened corners, close they cling,
Time cannot mar the tales they bring.
The past holds fast its guarded lore,
Of hidden truths and whispered hoar.

Each secret locked within its chest,
Where silence stands as solemn guest.
No prying hands may break the seal,
Of stories hidden, hearts conceal.

The layers thick, the mysteries cold,
In veils of time, their truths unfold.
Yet patient eyes and gentle hands,
May tease the threads of secret strands.

In quiet moments, shadows yield,
And truths once veiled are then revealed.
The whispers speak, the stories told,
And covered secrets lose their hold.

Envelope of Silence

Within a cloak of quietude,
The silence wraps its interlude.
An envelope of hush, complete,
Where thoughts and dreams in stillness meet.

The din and noise of day recede,
As silence sows its calming seed.
In tranquil space, the mind can roam,
Through whispers soft, it finds a home.

Each pause, a breath of unspoken words,
Where peace and calmness deeply gird.
The silence speaks in tones profound,
In every heartbeat's gentle sound.

The quiet spreads, its cover wide,
An envelope where souls confide.
In stillness, thoughts find clearer streams,
Within the silence, there are dreams.

Embrace the hush, the quiet grace,
In silence, find your sacred place.
For in the calm, the truths align,
And in the silence, one can shine.

Invisible Chains

Unseen, they bind the restless heart,
Invisible, they play their part.
In silence, they entwine and weave,
The ties that hold, yet none perceive.

The chains are forged from doubts and fears,
That echo through the quiet years.
Yet in their grip, there's strength to find,
A firmness in the soul's design.

Though bound by threads none see or grasp,
The spirit learns how tight to clasp.
For in the weight, there's growth and gain,
In silent struggles, wisdom’s chain.

Invisible, yet real as stone,
The chains we bear are often grown.
From whispers past, from shadows cast,
They shape the soul, they hold us fast.

But in the knowing, freedom lies,
To see the chains with clearer eyes.
Invisible though they may be,
We hold the key to set us free.

Veiled Insights

Beneath the shadows softly drift,
Where secrets slumber, dreams uplift.
Whispers weave through twilight's thread,
In hushed corners, truths are shed.

Layers cloak the tarnished gold,
Mysteries of the ages old.
Fleeting glimmers, knowledge glimpse,
Through the veil, the mind's eclipse.

Ephemeral the whispers' trace,
Hidden whispers interlace.
Silent truths in murmurs flow,
In the dark, we come to know.

Fractured light through curtains seep,
Ancient stories echo deep.
In the quiet, wisdom's song,
Edged in night, the insights throng.

Beneath the shadows' pale embrace,
Secrets find their resting place.
Through the veil, the world unveiled,
Ancient truths through whispers sailed.

Rooms of Silence

In the stillness of these walls,
Every echo gently falls.
Time suspended, whispers laced,
In the still rooms, silence traced.

Carved in quiet, secrets kept,
In corners where the shadows crept.
Windows softened by the past,
In the silence, shadows cast.

Moments drift on whispered winds,
Through the rooms where silence spins.
Echoes of the unheard phrase,
In the quiet, timeless gaze.

Each heartbeat in the silence clear,
Softly murmured, whispers near.
In these rooms, the quiet speaks,
Through the echoes, wisdom peaks.

Silent stories softly told,
In the rooms where stillness holds.
Veils of quiet softly fall,
In silence, ancient voices call.

All That is Hidden

Beneath the surface, shadows slide,
Secrets where the truths abide.
In the depths, the hidden gleam,
Silent as the midnight dream.

Murmured whispers, softly sown,
In the quiet, secrets grown.
Through the layers, darkness spins,
In the silence, truth begins.

Veils of night in mystery shroud,
In the stillness, whispers loud.
Shadows dance in hidden light,
Soft as whispers of the night.

Through the silence, echoes trace,
Patterns of the hidden place.
In the whispers, softly thrall,
In shadows' veil, we glimpse it all.

Beneath the surface, shadows lie,
Where the hidden stories cry.
In the darkness, softly tread,
Through the secrets, gently led.

Cryptic Chambers

In chambers deep, where shadows hide,
Whispers of the past reside.
Silence wraps the secrets bound,
In the dusk, the tales resound.

Labyrinth of echoes sway,
In the chambers, darkness play.
Murmurs weave through silent halls,
Mysteries echo from the walls.

Ancient voices softly weep,
In the chambers' quiet keep.
Through the silence, whispers throng,
In the dark, their secrets strong.

Silent paths the shadows trace,
In the chambers, time's embrace.
Ephemeral the whispers' gleam,
In the cryptic, truth redeem.

In chambers' depths, the secrets stay,
Where the hidden truths convey.
Through the silence softly tread,
In the chambers, softly led.

Concealed Wishes

In the heart's quiet folds,
Shadows play, secrets keep.
Yearning whispers, untold--
In silence, wishes seep.

In moonlight's tender grasp,
Dreams tenderly confide.
Stars in the night amass,
Desires, softly abide.

Within hope's fragile shell,
Longing sighs take their flight.
In the night, wishes swell,
As dreams dance with the night.

Hidden deep in the soul,
Passions softly ignite.
With each prayer, hearts feel whole,
Silent wishes alight.

In the unseen embrace,
Truth and dreams gently blend.
In shadows, they find place,
Where concealed wishes bend.

Cloaked Realities

In realms where silence reigns,
Unseen truths weave and wind.
Mysteries in refrain,
Secrets they seek, they find.

Masked by shadows so deep,
Hidden layers unfold.
Dreams in the dark, they sleep,
Midnight's tales, untold.

Behind the veils of night,
Realities lie concealed.
In the absence of light,
Hidden worlds are revealed.

Truths cloaked in mystery,
Their whispers lost to time.
In the dark, history,
Speaks in voiceless rhyme.

In shadows, they reside,
Stories both old and new.
Where secrets softly bide,
Cloaked truths come into view.

Behind Latches

Locks whisper tales of yore,
Keys that turn, secrets bare.
Stories hidden in lore,
Guarded with utmost care.

Behind latches, dreams wait,
In chambers dark, confined.
Patience alone, their fate,
Till freedom they may find.

Enclosed in silent rooms,
Longing in shadows cast.
In the still, hope resumes,
Tales of the quiet past.

Hearts bated, hold their breath,
Beyond gates, love entreats.
In the recess of death,
Yearning through silence beats.

Behind latches, life hums,
Silent harmonies blend.
In the hush, freedom comes,
Breaking through, dreams ascend.

Veiled Thoughts

In the mind's secret dance,
Thoughts weave in threads so fine.
Moments lost in a trance,
Dreams and ideas align.

Behind veils, wisdom hides,
Shadows of insights bold.
In silence, thought abides,
Stories softly unfold.

Thoughts in disguise, they play,
In the darkened recess.
Whispers at break of day,
Confide without duress.

Within the quiet mind,
Veiled thoughts gently reside.
Peace in the still, they find,
By inner light, they bide.

Deep in reflection's calm,
Spirit and thought entwine.
In the heart's tender psalm,
Veiled thoughts with dreams combine.

Secret Chambers

Behind the walls where shadows creep,
In chambers locked, a secret keep.
A whispered tale, a hidden flight,
In twilight's grasp, devoid of light.

The keyless lock, a mystery old,
In whispered legends, half-told.
Within the silence, echoes spin,
Secrets kept in boxes thin.

A curving stair, a silent gait,
To chambers locked by ancient fate.
No chart to guide, no map to show,
Where hidden secrets flow.

Silent guards, in statues grand,
Protect the past from mortal hand.
Echoes of a time gone by,
In secret chambers, whispers lie.

Dust collects on ancient lore,
In rooms untouched forevermore.
Here secrets sleep, forever sound,
In chambers deep, forever bound.

Forbidden Corners

In corners dark where light won't tread,
Whispered fears by shadows fed.
Of things unseen, and stories told,
In memories of the old.

A place where dreams and nightmares blend,
In corners where realities bend.
To venture close, a price to pay,
Forbidden paths where shadows play.

Secrets cloaked in mystery,
A hidden tale's history.
In corners dark, they softly wait,
To tempt a soul or test its fate.

A gust of wind, a whispered call,
In corners dark, do secrets fall.
Lurking there in shaded grace,
Time and space cannot erase.

Venture close and heed the creed,
Of corners dark where shadows feed.
A line unseen, to cross, a dare,
Beware the corners, venture where.

Obscured Realms

In realms unseen, beyond our eyes,
Lie hidden truths in veiled skies.
A world obscured by shadows deep,
Where unseen watchers nightly keep.

Mystic paths through forests dense,
A trail of whispers, not by chance.
Through veils of mist and shadowy beams,
We wander through forgotten dreams.

An ancient realm of roots and stone,
Where time’s forgotten seeds are sown.
In tangled webs, the secrets twine,
In obscured realms where shadows dine.

In twilight’s glow, we chance to see,
A fleeting glimpse of mystery.
A realm obscured by ancient grace,
Where hidden wonders find their place.

So listen close to nature's hum,
In obscured realms, the shadows come.
To those who seek, who dare to dream,
The secrets of the unseen gleam.

Protected Whispers

Whispers soft in silence kept,
Within hearts where secrets slept.
Protected by a sacred vow,
In echoes faint, they're sheltered now.

In hushed tones and gentle sighs,
Protected whispers softly lie.
Within each word, a hidden tale,
Of dreams and hopes they regale.

An oath once made, to guard, to shield,
Whispers kept, never revealed.
In shadows deep, they find their stay,
Protected from the light of day.

Guardians stand with watchful eyes,
Where whispers rise like silent cries.
In chambers deep, their echoes trace,
A dance of secrets, a guarded space.

In every heart, a chamber lies,
Where whispers sleep and secrets rise.
Protected whispers ever glow,
In silent hearts, they softly flow.

Locked Away

Behind the iron gates so tall,
A world unknown, away from all.
Secrets whisper through the air,
Hidden stories none would share.

The echoes of a thousand dreams,
Silent cries and muted schemes.
In darkness deep, they quietly stay,
The shadowed realm, all locked away.

A key forgotten, rusted chains,
Memories linger, like old refrains.
Time stands still within these walls,
Where no voice answers to calls.

The moonlight peeks through cracks unseen,
Painting pasts that might have been.
An enigma lost in night and day,
Life and love, forever locked away.

Hope whispers from the slightest breeze,
Awakening the silent pleas.
In hidden depths, light finds its way,
Unlocking dreams once locked away.

Quiet Havens

In places where the heart finds rest,
Where worries fade, the soul feels blessed.
Among the whispers of the trees,
The quiet havens calm the seas.

A gentle breeze, a soft refrain,
Erases thoughts of grief and pain.
In silent nooks, we find our peace,
A sanctuary where burdens cease.

The morning dew, on grassy beds,
Washes away the day's regrets.
The sunswept paths within these groves,
Nurture dreams and guide our roves.

Among the stars, beneath the night,
In tranquil dark or soft twilight,
We find a world so faint, so pure,
The quiet havens always cure.

With every breath, the calm surrounds,
Replacing chaos with gentle sounds.
In gentle arms, our hearts are craven,
Where lives are soothed in quiet havens.

Buried Feelings

Beneath the earth where shadows lie,
A world within where secrets sigh.
Emotions hidden from the day,
In the darkness, lost, they stay.

No sunlight warms these buried tales,
No wind to tell of life's travails.
Embracing silence in their keep,
Buried feelings rest, they sleep.

Forgotten songs, unheard desires,
In ashes cold, extinguished fires.
Yearnings fade, the echoes thin,
Lost among where dreams have been.

The whispers of a heart unseen,
In cloaked regrets and silver sheen.
Beneath the ground, they softly weep,
Buried feelings dig so deep.

Yet in the soil, hope might gleam,
A sprout of light, a budding dream.
Rising up from shadowed healings,
To unearth those buried feelings.

Secluded Moments

In hidden corners, time stands still,
Away from life's incessant drill.
Where silence wraps its quiet shroud,
A peaceful escape from the crowd.

In these moments, hearts can mend,
Both wounds and sorrow slowly tend.
A breath of ease, a calming sigh,
Where souls recluse, their peace is nigh.

The rustling leaves, the babbling brooks,
Nature speaks in hidden nooks.
Secluded from the worldly fright,
In solitude, we find the light.

A whispered prayer, a tranquil mind,
In moments far, the peace we find.
To disconnect, to softly blend,
Within ourselves, our time, we spend.

Each moment in this sacred space,
A gentle pause from life's long race.
Secluded moments, treasures glow,
In quietude, our spirits grow.

Reticent Reveries

In shadows deep, where whispers speak,
Silent dreams begin to creep.
A moonlit dance in twilight's grasp,
Through dawn's first light they softly pass.

Among the stars a secret's found,
Hushed tones in night, they do abound.
With every breath, a story told,
In quietude, the heart unfolds.

Softly tread where silence reigns,
In calm retreat, and none complain.
In gentle hush, the mind's released,
Where thoughts are free and fears deceased.

In hidden realms, a soul does bloom,
Beneath the sky in darkest plume.
Through veils of night, a mystic sight,
Reveries grow, in deepest night.

A whispered word, a silent vow,
In reverie, it's spoken now.
The quiet dreams that peaceful stay,
In night, they lead our hearts away.

Mysteries of the Mind

Unfathomed depths where thoughts reside,
In twilight zones, where dreams confide.
A realm obscure and undefined,
The secret paths inside the mind.

In corridors of shadowed grace,
Ideas form and interlace.
Through winding paths, enigmas spin,
Mysteries dwell deep within.

A labyrinth of mirrored halls,
Where echoes answer silent calls.
Each turn a phantasm to find,
In the myst'ries of the mind.

In silent spaces thoughts converge,
In whispered dreams on mental verge.
Hermetic truths in shadows wind,
Through the chambers of the mind.

Unlock the doors with keys of gold,
To secrets deep and tales untold.
Within, the treasures you shall find,
The myst'ries of the boundless mind.

Inward Reflections

In the stillness of the heart,
Inward journeys soft depart.
A mirror shows in silent hue,
Reflections of the inner view.

Each visage there a story tells,
In quietude where silence dwells.
Through mirrored glass, the soul can see,
The depths of our own mystery.

With every glance, a memory's called,
In solitude, the soul enthralled.
A quiet thought, a fleeting muse,
In inward peace, we softly lose.

Beneath the bounds of time and space,
In silent places, we embrace.
The essence of our inner light,
Reflected in the endless night.

In peaceful realms the heart is clear,
In solitude, there is no fear.
Reflecting inward we do find,
The beauty of the seeking mind.

Hushed Intimacies

In whispered breath, a secret shared,
In tender moments minds are bared.
Soft intimacies in the night,
In shadows dim and candlelight.

The quiet gaze, a touch so light,
Between the stars, in velvet night.
In secrecy, two hearts align,
In silent space, their loves define.

A hidden word, a gentle sigh,
Beneath the moon's attentive eye.
In hushed repose, the world withdraws,
Leaving two in nature's laws.

In silence soft, where love is bare,
Untold whispers fill the air.
In loving grace, with hearts entwined,
Two souls in hushed communion find.

In shadows faint and silken seams,
A world alights with fragile dreams.
In whispered vows, with love's decree,
The heart in hushed intimacy.

Confined Desires

Walls around, yet dreams fly high,
Behind closed doors, we reach the sky.
Silent whispers of what we crave,
In our hearts, they find a wave.

Bound by chains of doubts and fears,
Hidden wishes, silent tears.
In the shadows, passions burn,
Hoping one day they might turn.

Locked away, the world can't see,
The restless spirit yearning free.
In this cage, we softly sing,
Songs of hope and distant spring.

Within our souls, a fire glows,
Where it leads us, no one knows.
Desire's furnace, secret heat,
Burns within, discreet, discreet.

Confined for now, but not for long,
These desires forever strong.
In the quiet, dreams will rise,
Touch the earth, and kiss the skies.

Private Nook

In a corner, quiet, still,
Lies a refuge from the thrill.
Softly lit by twilight's grace,
It's our own secluded space.

Hidden from the world's demand,
Here we rest with hand in hand.
Safe within this private nook,
No need for another look.

Whispers shared in hushed delight,
Dreams take flight into the night.
Heartfelt moments, pure and sweet,
In this space where shadows meet.

Bound by neither time nor place,
Lost within a tender embrace.
In this nook, no fears reside,
Just the warmth felt inside.

Rest we find in this tight hug,
Sheltered in like an old rug.
Private nook, we cherish so,
A secret place where love can grow.

Enshrouded Secrets

Wrapped in night, the secrets lie,
Hidden from the prying eye.
Enshrouded deep within our souls,
Whispered truths and shadowed goals.

Veiled in darkness, they reside,
In quiet spaces where they hide.
Silent keepers of our dreams,
Flowing with life's shadowed streams.

In the hush, they softly speak,
Words profound and voices meek.
Secrets held in gentle trust,
Guarded well, as all things must.

In the shadows, lies unfold,
Stories hidden, tales untold.
Within the hearth of silent grace,
Secrets find their resting place.

Though concealed, they form our core,
Mysteries that we adore.
Enshrouded secrets, vast and grand,
Shape the heart and guide the hand.

Sequestered Scenes

Withdrawn from the hectic blaze,
In quietude, we spend our days.
Sequestered scenes so close and dear,
Rippled streams, reflections clear.

From the world, a soft retreat,
Nature's grace at our feet.
Gentle winds and rustling leaves,
Lend a solace that relieves.

Amid the hush, we find our peace,
In these moments, time does cease.
Sequestered scenes, a sacred space,
A tender, calm, intimate place.

Here we wander, lost in thought,
In seclusion, comfort sought.
Wrapped in stillness, feeling free,
Nature's hand is our decree.

Sequestered scenes, a world apart,
Healing balm for weary heart.
In their hold, we find our soul,
Wholeness in the quiet's role.

Shadows of the Past

In the twilight of old memories,
Whispers drift on gentle breeze,
Footsteps echo of times long gone,
In shadows past where we're drawn.

Faded photographs, sepia tones,
Stories carved in weathered stones,
Songs of yesteryears softly play,
In the hush of end-of-day.

Laughter rings from shadowy halls,
Silent are the empty walls,
A tapestry of joy and tears,
Woven through the countless years.

Ghostly hands that gently brush,
Timeless voices break the hush,
In dreams we meet, our souls avast,
Wandering shadows of the past.

The moments lost, yet here they stay,
In heart's deep chamber, tucked away,
Though time moves on, shadows last,
Eternal figures in the past.

Veiled Lies

Behind the mask, deceits reside,
Truths obscured, secrets tide,
Eyes may glimmer, hiding fears,
Veiled lies whisper in our ears.

Perceptions twist in shadowed light,
Day and night in endless fight,
Promises made on fragile threads,
Bitter truths on which we dread.

Candles flicker in twilight grey,
Shadows dance in cryptic play,
Words like silk, yet daggers hide,
In the heart where veiled lies bide.

Trust once given, now returned,
Lessons harshly learned and learned,
Heartfelt pleas, yet cold replies,
Wrapped within those veiled lies.

Truth will find its way to gleam,
Through the cracks of broken dream,
In the light of morning's rise,
Revealing all the veiled lies.

Unopened Letters

In a drawer, long lain untouched,
Rest unread, their words so clutched,
Unopened letters, tales untold,
Mysteries in envelopes fold.

Ink on paper, heart's deep plea,
Feelings locked from you and me,
Sealed with hope, with tears confined,
Innocence of hearts combined.

Day by day, as seasons pass,
Memories in each line amass,
Yet they lie, just whispers still,
Awaiting time to break their chill.

Hands that wrote in fevered rush,
Now are still, quiet hush,
Words of love, or perhaps regret,
Thoughts we never can forget.

Shall we open? Dare we read?
Fragile truths our hearts would heed,
Unopened letters, silent keep,
Eternal dreams in paper sleep.

Gated Secrets

Behind iron gates, secrets keep,
In silent guard, their whispers sleep,
Creaking hinges, tales untold,
Mysteries within unfold.

In the garden, shadows play,
Sunlight fades and night holds sway,
Voices lost in yesteryear,
Haunted echoes fill the ear.

Paths untrodden, overgrown,
Leads to truths we've never known,
Locked away with ancient keys,
Hidden under timeless trees.

Silent watchers, stone and moss,
Hold the tales of love and loss,
Histories carved in darkened wood,
Not revealed, but understood.

Somber moon and stars alight,
Guard the secrets through the night,
Gates are closed, but in our dreams,
We glimpse the past in shadowed gleams.

Void of Unspoken

In whispers on the twilight breeze,
A silence wraps, it never flees,
The void where spoken words should be,
A realm of thought, eternally.

Unseen, the echoes softly trail,
Through empty spaces, whispering tales,
Yet none disturb the tranquil night,
Where silence reigns, and hearts take flight.

Within this void, the secrets soar,
They dance upon an unseen floor,
An eloquence in quiet shown,
A language of the soul alone.

No tongue can speak the silent lore,
It's written in the stars that soar,
In breaths unvoiced, a truth profound,
In silence, where our dreams are found.

A symphony of hushed repose,
In quiet, hidden beauty grows,
Embrace the void, the unspoken dreams,
In silence, find what truly gleams.

Silent Walls

Within these walls, a quiet hum,
Of stories old and those to come,
They whisper secrets of the past,
In silence, friendships forged to last.

The creak of floor, the sigh of beams,
A house alive with silent dreams,
Each room a world, a tale untold,
In shadows, histories unfold.

They speak of laughter, speak of tears,
Of whispered hopes, and hidden fears,
A language silent, yet so clear,
In quiet moments, all appear.

The walls they breathe, with life imbued,
In tranquil silence, solitude,
Yet full of love, and warmth they bring,
In stillness, hear their murmuring.

Through silent halls, the ghosts of time,
Walk hand in hand, in perfect rhyme,
The beauty of the walls' soft grace,
In silence, find a loving space.

Veil of Privacy

A curtain falls, a veil is drawn,
In shadows deep before the dawn,
A sacred space, where thoughts can flee,
In quietude, there’s privacy.

The world outside, a distant hum,
Within, the heartbeats softly drum,
A fortress built of silent thread,
A haven where the soul is fed.

No prying eyes, no listening ear,
In solitude, what we hold dear,
A space where whispers softly fade,
In private reverie we wade.

Behind the veil, our dreams take flight,
They dance in shades of softest light,
Each thought a star in silent skies,
In privacy, the spirit sighs.

In stillness, find the self anew,
Where every wish, and hope is true,
A veil drawn close, a world apart,
In privacy, lies the heart.

Shadows of Concealment

In shadows where the secrets lay,
A world unseen, by light of day,
They whisper truths, in deepest night,
In darkness, all is brought to light.

Behind the veil of shadowed hue,
Exist the dreams we never knew,
They hide away, in secret folds,
In silence, every tale unfolds.

Those shadows dance, along the wall,
They mimic life, then softly fall,
In concealment, they find grace,
In darkness, there’s a sacred space.

No eye can pierce, no ear can hear,
The hidden truths that do appear,
In shadows, life is softly spun,
A silent tale, that’s never done.

In twilight’s grasp, the shadows reign,
They guard the secrets, joy and pain,
In concealment, find what’s true,
In shadows, lies the heart anew.

Forbidden Thoughts

In shadows deep, where whispers tread,
Thoughts unspoken, fears unfed,
Hidden cries beneath the veil,
Secrets dark that tips the scale.

Behind each smile, a tangled web,
Words unuttered, lies we've bred,
Silent screams in muted night,
Painted faces, hearts in flight.

In darkest corners, minds do stray,
To paths uncharted, far away,
Dreams forbidden, passions bold,
Stories left, untold, untold.

Eyes may glisten, truth concealed,
Feelings locked, never revealed,
In the vaults of souls confined,
Forbidden thoughts, now intertwined.

Through veils of dusk, we dare not peek,
For shadows hold the truth we seek,
Yet in the silence, courage builds,
To speak the thoughts our hearts do yield.

Curtained Dreams

Behind the curtain, dreams do dance,
Whispers float in twilight's trance,
Unseen worlds where wishes rest,
In the silence, hope’s impressed.

Through the veil, the mind does play,
Chasing night where shadows stay,
Dreams unspoken, secret flights,
Through the ebon, starry nights.

Curtains close, and dreams arise,
Rainbow hues in moonlit skies,
Ephemeral, yet burning bright,
Fleeting as the morning light.

Hush, the whispers softly sing,
Of dreams with gilded, fragile wing,
Curtains drawn, yet hearts afire,
Yearning, longing, deep desire.

In the quiet, dreams unfurl,
Curtained from the waking world,
In that space where silence beams,
Woven tight are curtained dreams.

Invisible Threads

Invisible threads, we cannot see,
Bind our hearts in mystery,
Threads of love, of joy and pain,
Woven tight in life's refrain.

Unseen hands that weave our fate,
Spinning stories, hearts elate,
Connections made without a word,
Silent bonds that go unheard.

In the dance of life, we find,
Threads of fate that intertwine,
Binding us through space and time,
Invisible, yet so sublime.

Through the years, these threads endure,
Ties that hold, steadfast and pure,
Guiding us through storm and stress,
Invisible threads that bless.

In the web of life, they blend,
Threads unseen that never end,
Binding souls in unseen bands,
Invisible threads in gentle hands.

Under the Surface

Under the surface, secrets lie,
Silent whispers, hidden sigh,
Beneath the calm, a storm does brew,
Truths unknown to me and you.

In shadows deep, where light is sparse,
Dwells the heart with hidden scars,
Eyes may sparkle, faces gleam,
Yet below, lies unseen dream.

Underneath, the currents flow,
Darkened waters, undertow,
Masked by smiles, the pain remains,
Silent tears, like hidden rains.

Swirling deep in unseen space,
Emotions run, they leave no trace,
Beneath the surface, shadows dance,
Silent, unseen, their mournful trance.

Seek the depths where truth resides,
In the silent, hidden tides,
For under the surface, souls ignite,
Revealing secrets in the night.

Hidden Yearnings

In silent nights, where dreams entwine,
Hearts whisper secrets, soft, benign.
A yearning kept behind closed doors,
Emotions stir, forever soar.

Eyes that glance, but never meet,
A love that's hidden, bittersweet.
Unspoken words, a timid plea,
In shadows, hearts long to be free.

Silent songs of soul’s desire,
Burn within, a quiet fire.
Fingers reach, but never touch,
Longing aches, it means so much.

Distant stars, they seem so near,
Yet love's a tale wrapped up in fear.
In the twilight, hearts remain,
Dreams untold, a silent chain.

Beneath the surface, deep within,
A love concealed, in shadows thin.
One day, perhaps, they'll find their way,
From hidden yearnings, hearts won’t stray.

Cryptic Spaces

Between the lines of life's embrace,
Exist the realms of cryptic space.
Mysteries veiled in silent dust,
In truth unknown, we place our trust.

Whispered thoughts in quiet hall,
Secrets linger, none can call.
Echoes of the bygone days,
Haunt the mind in cryptic ways.

Shadows play in twilight's hue,
Revealing worlds we never knew.
Paths diverge and intertwine,
In the cryptic, all align.

Veiled in darkness, wrapped in night,
Cryptic spaces hide from sight.
Yet within, a silent spark,
Guides the wandering through the dark.

Unseen realms where thoughts reside,
Cryptic spaces, none can hide.
Journey through their mystic maze,
Lost in these, our minds do daze.

Whispered Walls

In ancient halls with whispered walls,
History's secrets gently call.
Voices soft from time gone by,
Echo in the silent sky.

Walls that murmur tales of yore,
Of love and loss, and so much more.
Memories etched in stone and clay,
Guarded whispers, night and day.

In the stillness, they confide,
Stories lost, within they hide.
Their whispers are a silent guide,
To hearts that seek, and souls that bide.

Listen close, you'll hear the past,
In whispered walls, forever cast.
Their secrets tell of dreams untold,
Of hearts once young, now growing old.

Through the years and through the tears,
Whispered walls will quell our fears.
In their silence, truths unfold,
Stories rich and secrets bold.

Passageways of Silence

Through passageways of silent streams,
We wander lost in tangled dreams.
Silent whispers guide our way,
Through the night and into day.

In corridors of time and space,
We journey at a quiet pace.
Echoes fill the vacant halls,
Each step a story, each footfall.

Unheard breaths, they intertwine,
With silence deep, a sacred sign.
From shadows cast, we draw the light,
In silent passageways of night.

Moving through the still refrain,
In silence, none can see the pain.
Yet here we find a tranquil grace,
In these silent, boundless space.

Passageways where thoughts are free,
Silence holds the hidden key.
Within their depths, we find our song,
In silent passageways, we belong.

Secret Lives

In shadows where the secrets lie,
Beyond the glimmer and the sigh,
A world unseen yet voices call,
Hidden tales, they stand so tall.

Invisible threads, we weave them tight,
In whispers that evade the light,
An echo through the silent night,
Our secret lives, they take their flight.

Masks we wear, in subtle grace,
Concealing stories, every face,
Behind closed doors, our dreams reside,
In secret lives, we take our stride.

Unrevealed, undetected trace,
Still as winds in boundless space,
A diary of the soul, confined,
In every heart, a world combined.

In silent coves, in veiled refrain,
The secret lives possess no chain,
Beneath the surface, whispers thrive,
Eternal dance, we are alive.

Whispers in the Hallway

Through the corridors of time they glide,
Silent echoes, side by side,
In shadowed corners, softly hide,
Whispers in the hallway bide.

Ghostly murmurs quietly chime,
Tales untold from another clime,
In empty spaces, secrets rhyme,
A dance within the fleeting prime.

Behind each door, a hidden plea,
A story whispered, wild and free,
A trace of magic, we might see,
In whispers held, the mystery.

In hushed tones the walls will keep,
The promises that shadows reap,
In every crack and crevice deep,
The whispers in the hallway sleep.

Voices fade yet leave a mark,
In twilight's slow advancing dark,
The whispers in the hallway spark,
A haunting song, an ember's arc.

Veiled Emotions

Beneath a smile, a tear will hide,
Within the heart, emotions ride,
A storm inside, a gentle tide,
In veiled emotions, worlds collide.

Eyes that sparkle, hinting pain,
A summer's sun or autumn's rain,
Behind the veil, there lies a strain,
Unseen, unheard, the sweet refrain.

Silent screams within the mind,
A whisper only shadows find,
In every glance, emotions bind,
Veiled in silence, undefined.

In laughter's echo, sorrow sleeps,
A secret vow the silence keeps,
In veiled emotions, heart still weeps,
A promise in the darkness creeps.

Masked and hidden, truth will roam,
In silent lulls, it finds its home,
In veiled emotions, we become,
A symphony of silent hum.

Curtain of Secrecy

Drawn apart, the curtain sways,
In hidden realms, where shadows play,
A secret world in muted grays,
Behind the veil, the secrets stay.

In whispered winds, the tales unfold,
A tapestry of dreams untold,
Beneath the threads of darkened gold,
The hidden truths, they silently hold.

Secrets held, in chambers deep,
Beneath the whispers, shadows sleep,
A silent watch the guardians keep,
In veiled realms where spirits leap.

Behind the curtain, lives unseen,
A dance of shadows, in between,
In hushed tones, a sacred scene,
The curtain of secrecy, a serene.

With every fold, a tale concealed,
In shadows' grasp, the truth revealed,
A sacred bond, forever sealed,
Within the secrets, hearts are healed.

Printed in the USA
CPSIA information can be obtained
at www.ICGtesting.com
LVHW011140080824
787694LV00002B/213

9 789916 763490